Coding with ScratchJr

By Adrienne Matteson

CHERRY LAKE Publishing

Published in the United States of America by
Cherry Lake Publishing
Ann Arbor, Michigan
www.cherrylakepublishing.com

Series Adviser: Kristin Fontichiaro
Reading Adviser: Marla Conn, MS, Ed., Literacy specialist,
Read-Ability, Inc.
Photo Credits: Cover, Wesley Fryer / tinyurl.com/gql2ldo /
CC BY 2.0; all other images by Adrienne Matteson

Library of Congress Cataloging-in-Publication Data
Names: Matteson, Adrienne, author.
Title: Coding with ScratchJr / by Adrienne Matteson.
Other titles: Coding with Scratch Jr | 21st century skills innovation library.
  Makers as innovators.
Description: Ann Arbor, Michigan : Cherry Lake Publishing, [2017] | Series: Makers
  as innovators junior | Series: 21st century skills innovation library | Audience: K to
  grade 3. | Includes bibliographical references and index.
Identifiers: LCCN 2016032413| ISBN 9781634721868 (lib. bdg.) | ISBN 9781634723183
  (pbk.) | ISBN 9781634722520 (pdf) | ISBN 9781634723848 (ebook)
Subjects: LCSH: Scratch (Computer program language)—Juvenile literature. | Computer
  programming—Juvenile literature. | Programming languages (Electronic computers)—
  Juvenile literature.
Classification: LCC QA76.52 .M3835 2017 | DDC 005.26/2—dc23 LC record available
  at https://lccn.loc.gov/2016032413

Cherry Lake Publishing would like to acknowledge the work of the Partnership for
21st Century Learning. Please visit *www.p21.org* for more information.

Printed in the United States of America
Corporate Graphics

A Note to Adults: Please review the instructions for the activities in this book before allowing children to do them. Be sure to help them with any activities you do not think they can safely complete on their own.

A Note to Kids: Be sure to ask an adult for help with these activities when you need it. Always put your safety first!

Table of Contents

ScratchJr is easy to use. It is also a lot of fun!

Who Can Write Computer Programs?

Our world is full of computers. Computers are in phones, watches, and even cars! Every computer works by following **programs**. Have you ever thought about creating your own computer programs? You could make a computer do whatever you want. One great way to get started is to use something called ScratchJr.

You can create programs in ScratchJr by dragging colorful blocks around on the touch screen of a tablet computer.

What Is ScratchJr?

ScratchJr is a **programming language** made just for kids. It works on iPads and other tablet computers. With ScratchJr, you can create stories and games for your friends to play. You will also learn how to think like a computer programmer!

What Is a Programming Language?

A programming language is a set of words, **symbols**, and rules. It is used to write **instructions** for a computer. There are a lot of programming languages. ScratchJr is just one of them!

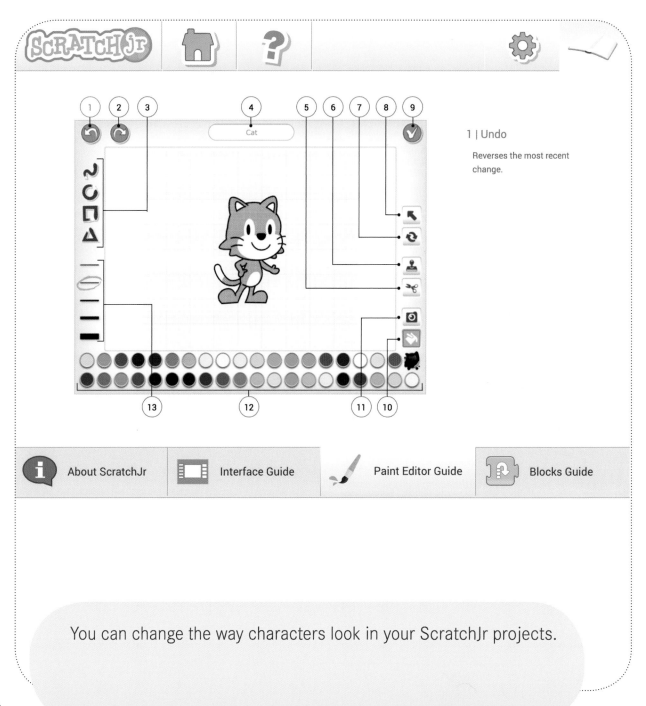

1 | Undo

Reverses the most recent change.

About ScratchJr   Interface Guide   Paint Editor Guide   Blocks Guide

You can change the way characters look in your ScratchJr projects.

How Does ScratchJr Work?

A ScratchJr project is made up of three parts. These are characters, backgrounds, and **code blocks**. Characters are the things in your project that move and talk. Backgrounds are the pictures that set the scene for a story. Code blocks tell your characters and backgrounds what to do.

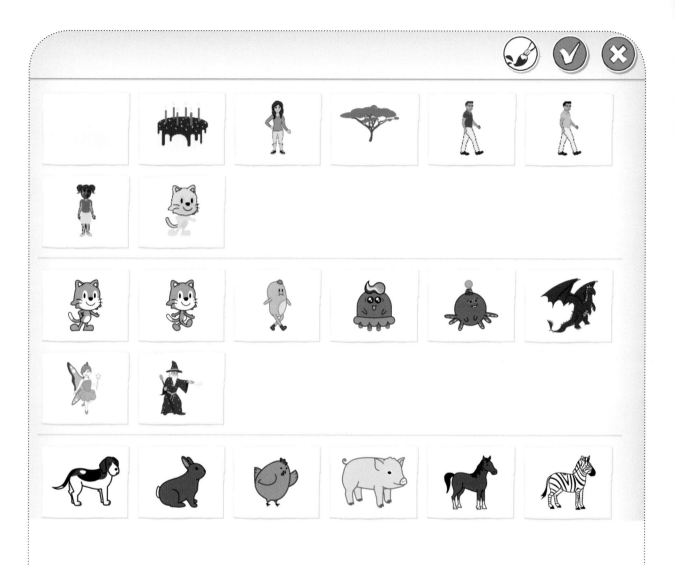

ScratchJr comes with many characters you can choose from.

Characters

A character is anything in your project that moves, speaks, or changes somehow. Characters can be people and animals. A character might also be a rock or a cupcake. It can be an object another character picks up. Even a star twinkling in the sky can be a character in your project.

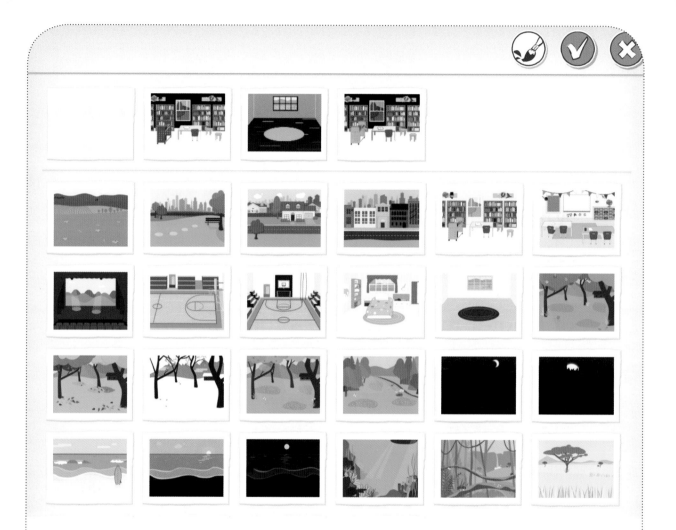

There is a background for any project you can think of in ScratchJr.

Backgrounds

Where does your story take place? There are lots of backgrounds to choose from. Don't worry if they aren't the right color. Every background can be changed to fit your ideas. Just tap on the paintbrush when you pick a background. Then use the drawing tools to make it just right.

Think About It!

You can use up to four backgrounds per project. Can you think of a story to tell that takes place in more than one setting?

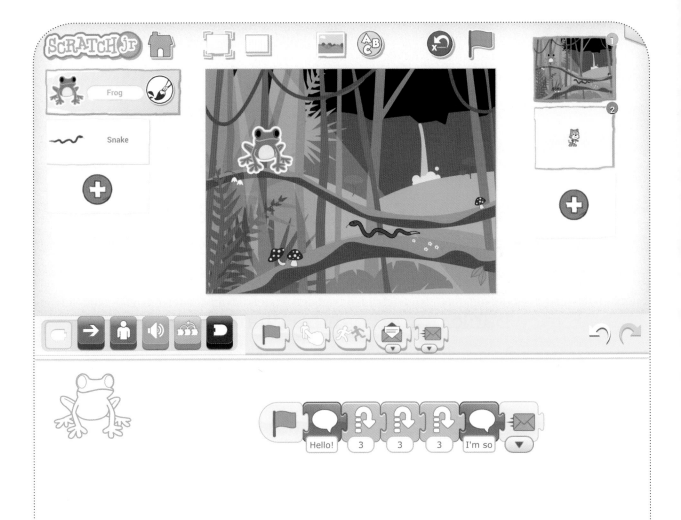

All programs start with a yellow block.

Color-Coded Code Blocks

How do you know which code blocks to use? Blocks are color coded to help you remember what they do.

- Yellow blocks begin a program.
- Red blocks end it.
- Blue blocks move characters around the screen.
- Purple blocks change the characters' looks.
- Green blocks let you add sounds.

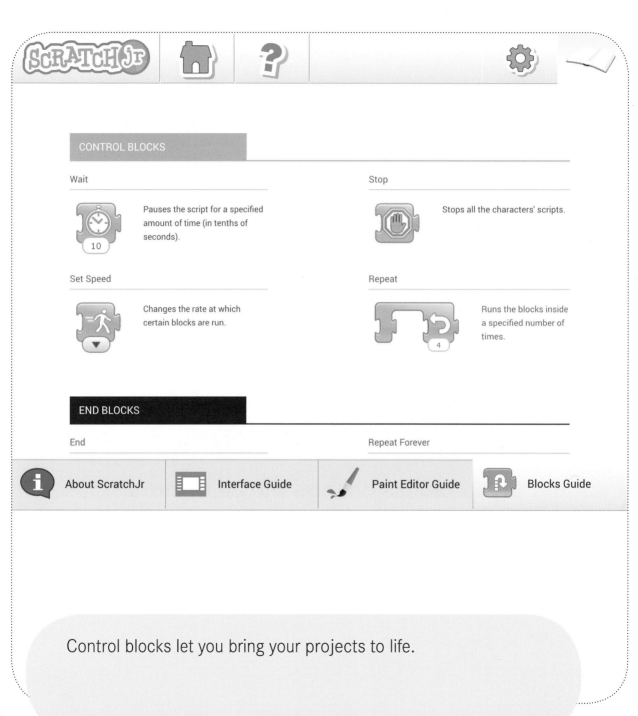

CONTROL BLOCKS

Wait

Pauses the script for a specified amount of time (in tenths of seconds).

10

Stop

Stops all the characters' scripts.

Set Speed

Changes the rate at which certain blocks are run.

Repeat

Runs the blocks inside a specified number of times.

4

END BLOCKS

End

Repeat Forever

About ScratchJr   Interface Guide   Paint Editor Guide   Blocks Guide

Control blocks let you bring your projects to life.

Control Blocks

Orange code blocks are called control blocks. Orange blocks are in charge! Do you want Scratch Cat to spin around five times? Use the orange "Repeat" block. Do you want an elephant to lose a race? Use the orange "Set Speed" block to make him move slowly.

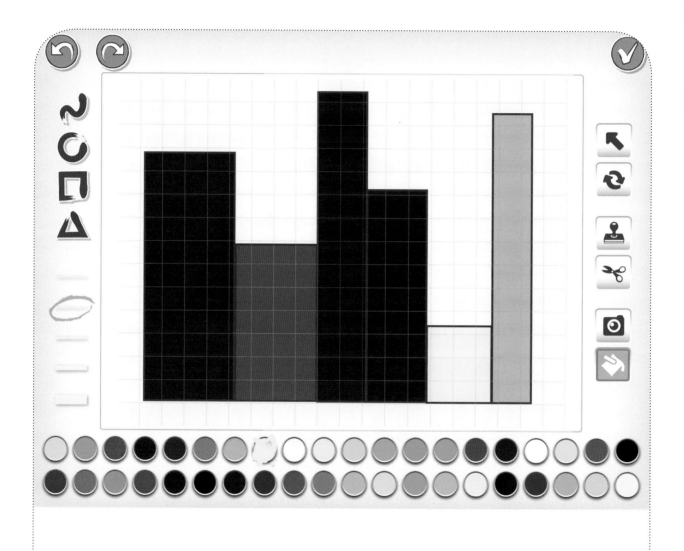

Try creating your own colorful backgrounds.

Make It Your Own!

Can't find the background you want in the ScratchJr **gallery**? No problem! Use the paint editor to create your own. The paint editor has tools for filling in color, drawing by hand, and adding shapes. You can even use the camera to add your own face to a character.

Can I Save the Characters and Backgrounds I Make?

Yes! Every character and background you create is saved to the gallery. This means you can use it again in other projects. If friends share their projects with you, their characters and backgrounds will be saved, too.

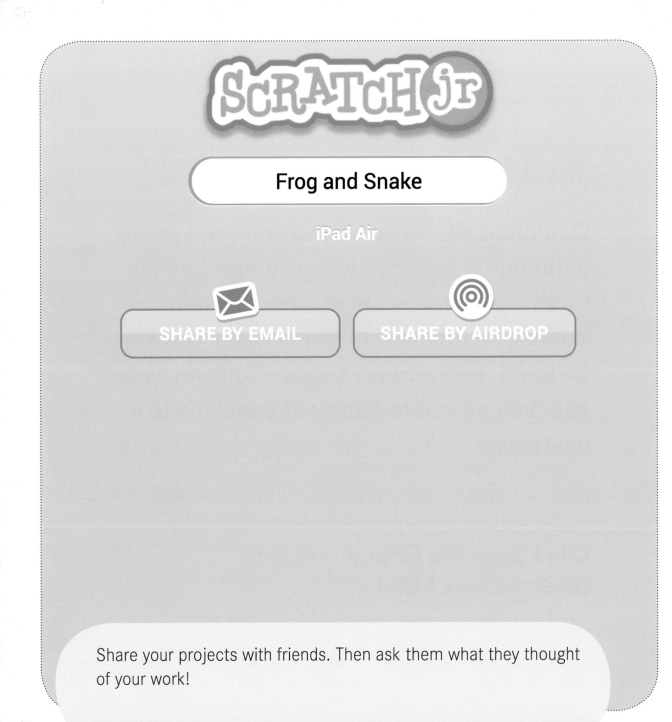

Share your projects with friends. Then ask them what they thought of your work!

Sharing Your Project

When you finish a project, you can share it! ScratchJr projects can be shared two ways. One way is to send them to friends through e-mail. The other way only works with iPads. You can use the AirDrop feature to send your project from one iPad to another. Ask an adult to help you before sharing anything. Congratulations! You made a program!

Glossary

code blocks (KODE BLAHKS) the smallest pieces of a ScratchJr program, each containing a single instruction

gallery (GAL-ur-ee) a picture list of all the characters or backgrounds available to use in ScratchJr

instructions (in-STRUHK-shuhnz) directions on how to do something

programming language (PROH-gram-ing LANG-wij) a set of words, symbols, and rules used to write instructions for a computer

programs (PROH-gramz) instructions that tell a computer how to complete a task

symbols (SIM-buhlz) designs or objects that stand for something else

Find Out More

Book

Bers, Marina Umaschi, and Mitchel Resnick. *The Official ScratchJr Book: Help Your Kids Learn to Code!* San Francisco: No Starch Press, 2016.

Web Sites

Scratch

scratch.mit.edu

When you are ready, make more complicated programs using ScratchJr's big brother, Scratch.

ScratchJr

www.scratchjr.org

Learn all about using ScratchJr, watch videos, and try practice activities.

Index

About the Author

Adrienne Matteson is a school librarian. She spends most of her days playing with robots and helping her students write programs about unicorns.